Audubon Birds
COLORING BOOK

Patricia J. Wynne

Dover Publications, Inc.
Mineola, New York

This beautiful coloring book features thirty-one detailed illustrations of birds of North America as depicted by the great painter and naturalist John James Audubon (1785–1851). Carefully and accurately reproduced, these plates feature such remarkable creatures as the white pelican, great horned owl, and the tundra swan. It also includes images of several extinct species, including the great auk, Carolina parakeet, and passenger pigeon. Each bird is identified in a caption, and the perforated pages make displaying your finished artwork easy.

Copyright

Copyright © 2017 by Dover Publications, Inc.
All rights reserved.

Bibliographical Note

Audubon Birds Coloring Book is a new work, first published by Dover Publications, Inc., in 2017.

International Standard Book Number

ISBN-13: 978-0-486-81380-6
ISBN-10: 0-486-81380-0

Manufactured in the United States by LSC Communications
81380004   2017
www.doverpublications.com

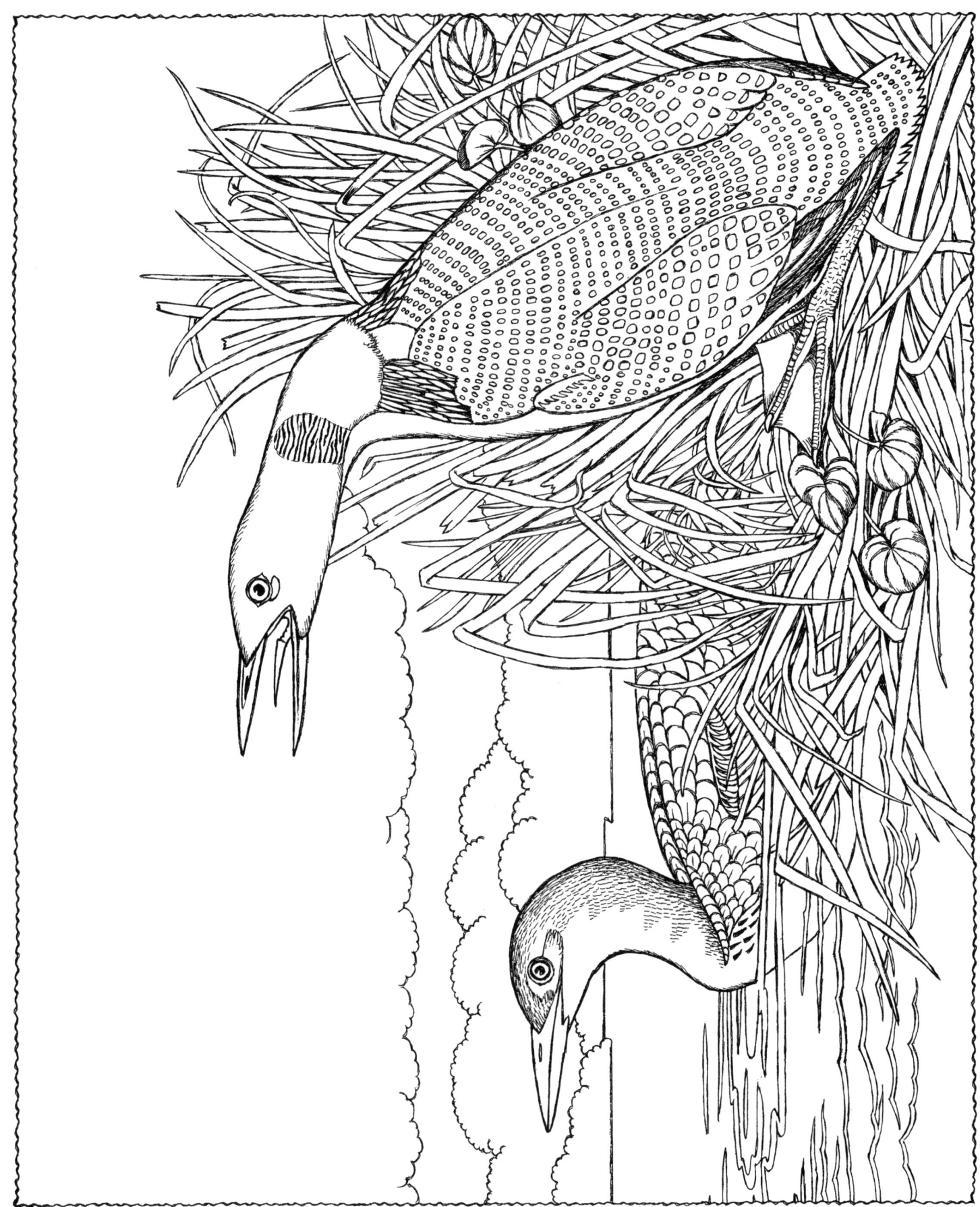

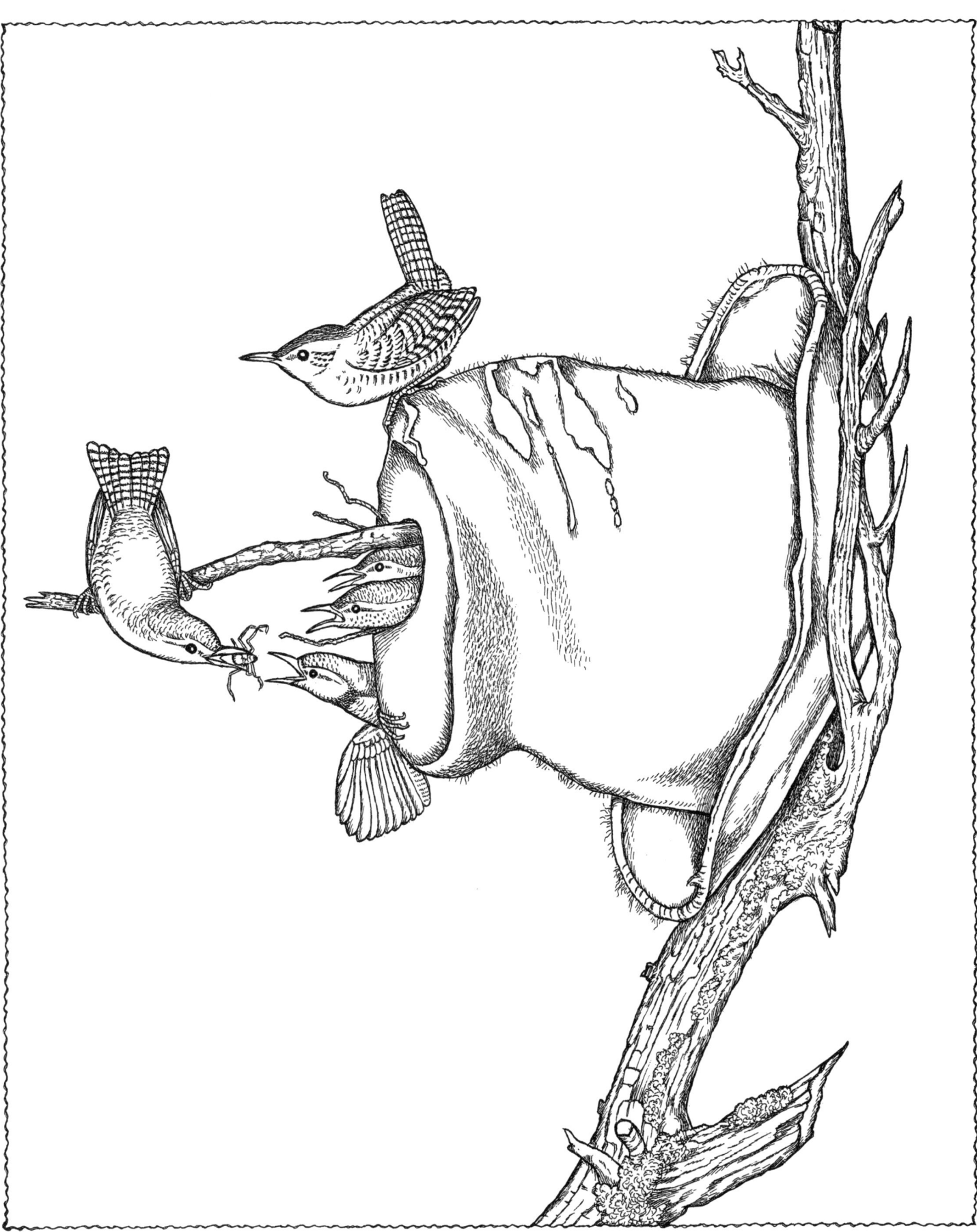

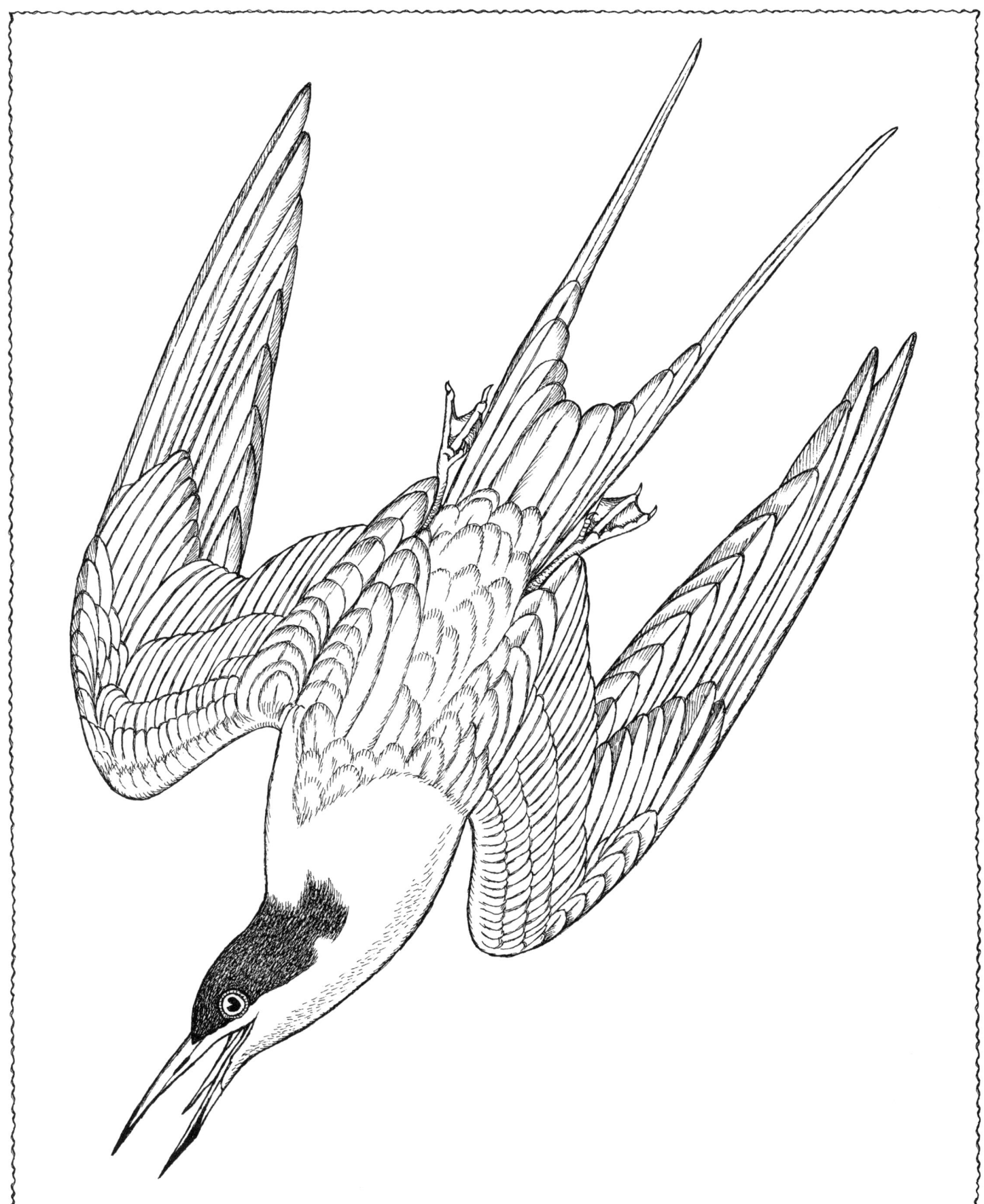

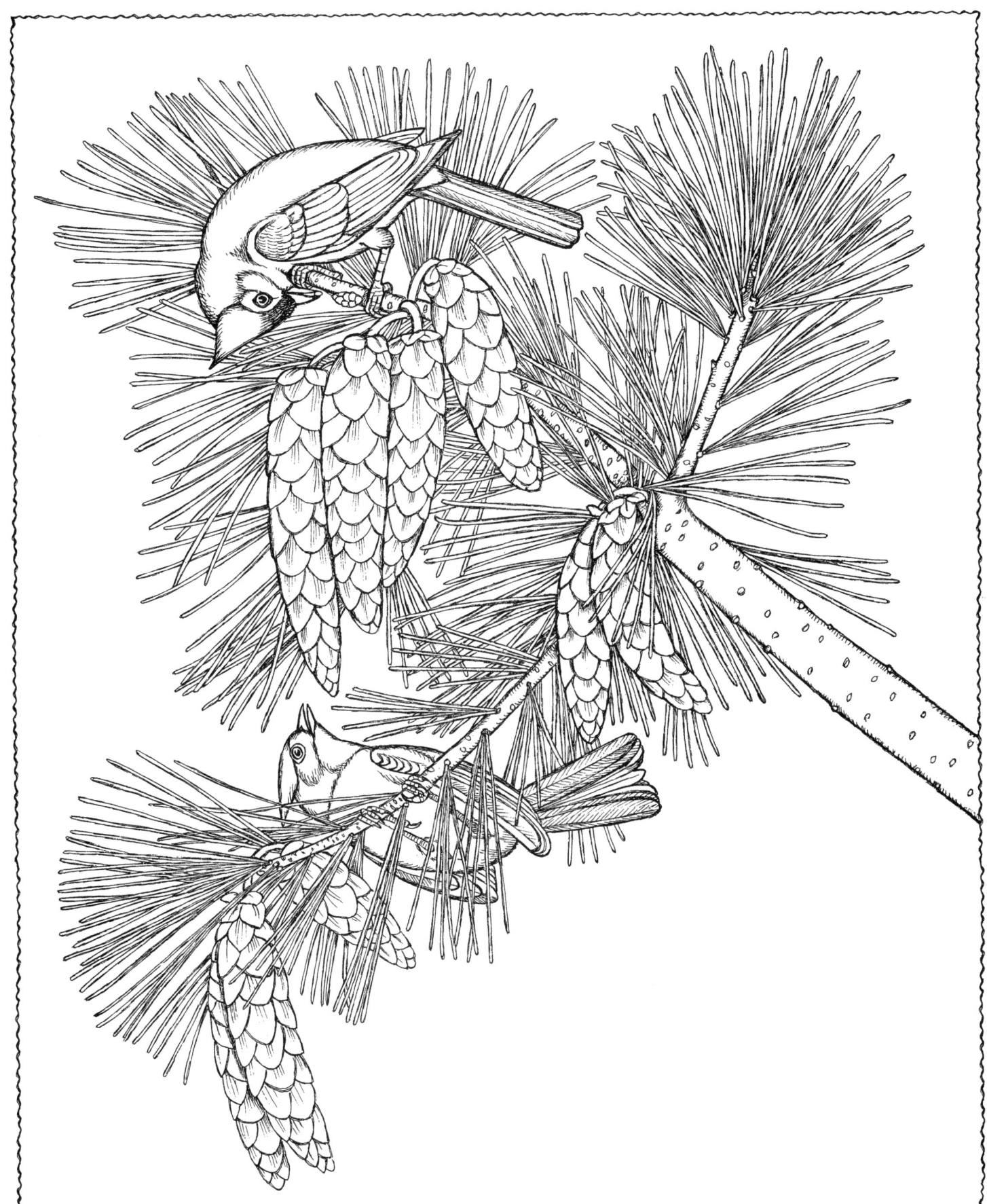

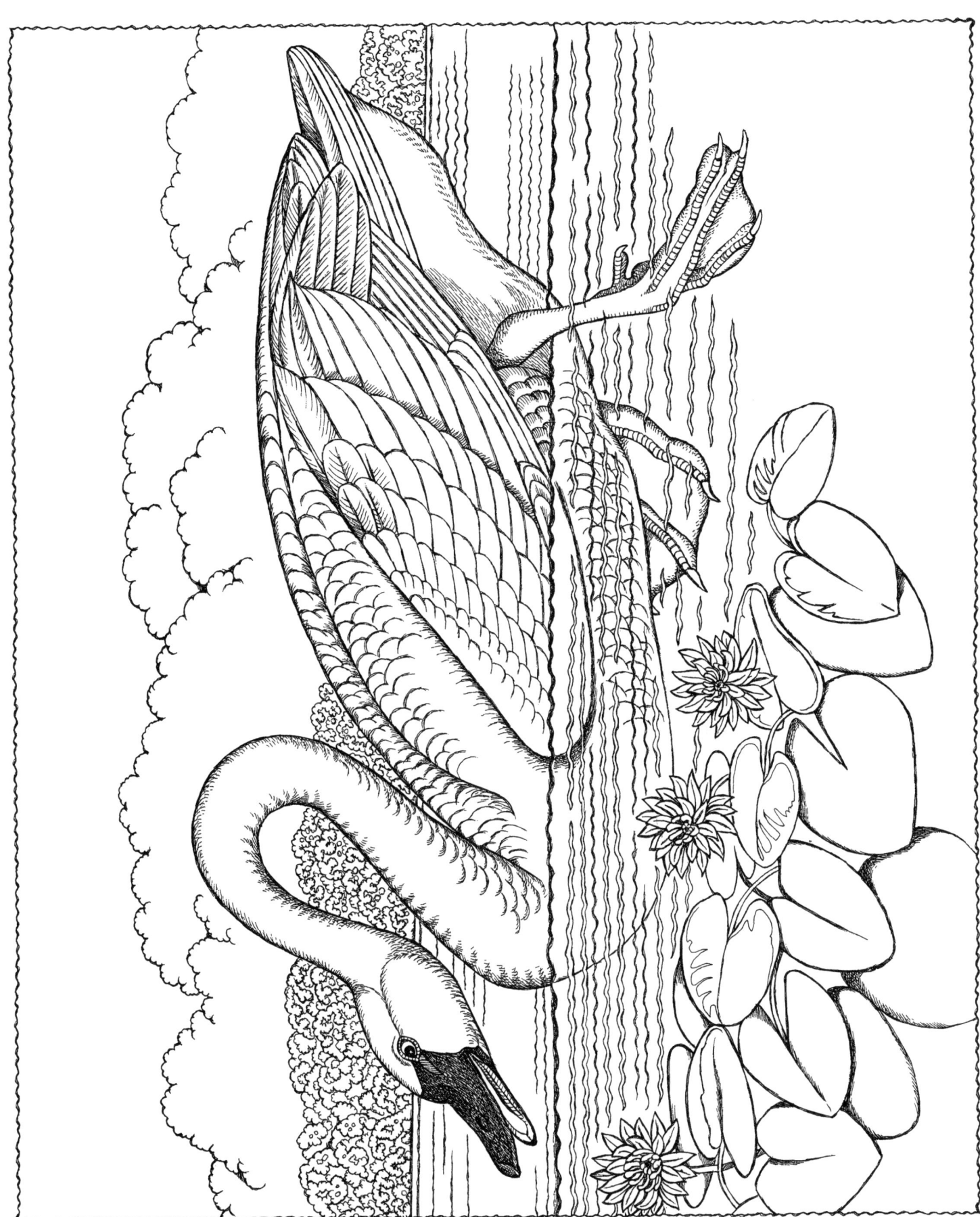